Table of Contents

Author's Introduction

I've been responsible for creating, setting up and helping to manage various websites that use WordPress. I've written this book to hopefully answer the many questions I've received about the day to day management of a WordPress website.

I wrote this book as I've found many of the books covering WordPress are aimed more at the developers, and go into technical details, rather then covering the essentials for the day to day management of a website. A lot of people are looking for a book that shows them how to manage their website, without being scared away by technical details!

Perhaps a web designer created a website for you, and you are not sure how to update content, or you have started a new job and need to know how to manage your website. You certainly don't want to be scared away by technical details! This book is for you.

Consider this book your manual on updating and managing your website!

This third edition includes updated pictures and information – one most notable change to WordPress since the previous two editions is the new Blocks editor for editing pages/blogs, and this is covered, along with the original classic editor.

If you have comments, questions or suggestions about this book – or if you are looking for help with your website and would like to discuss freelance opportunities, send me an e-mail: **simon@libraryplayer.co.uk**

Finally, I would like to thank Jim Simpson (**www.thevintageyears.co.uk**) and Gordon Wright for the screenshots and examples from their websites.

I hope this book proves valuable in helping you look after your website!

Simon Pittman
2nd October 2019

E-mail simon@libraryplayer.co.uk
Website www.libraryplayer.co.uk
Facebook www.facebook.com/LibraryPlayer
Twitter www.twitter.com/LibraryPlayer

What is WordPress?

What is WordPress?

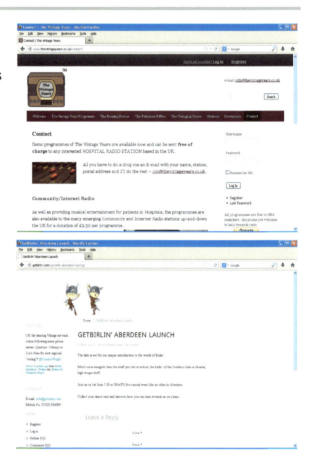

WordPress is a content management system that allows you to set up a website that can then easily be updated. Simply install WordPress to your hosting, set it up and customize it and you then have a website you can easily edit and update.

While originally created for blogs, it can be used for other types of websites too.

WordPress is available and can be used free of charge. It can be downloaded from **www.wordpress.org** – and some web hosting companies offer to install it for you (otherwise you need to install it manually). Before buying hosting, check that they support WordPress, if you are not sure them an e-mail and ask.

Many organisations, individuals, small charities and large organisations use WordPress for their website.

With WordPress you will find that editing a page is as easy as editing a document in Microsoft Word.

WordPress versus WordPress.com

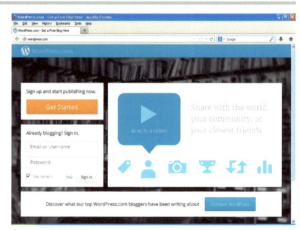

Something that confuses a lot of people is the difference between WordPress and WordPress.com.

This book covers the WordPress software available from WordPress.org, that you install and set up on your own web server or hosting.

There is also a blogging website called WordPress.com where you can set up a blog for free – hosted on the WordPress.com website. Although they use the same WordPress software this is separate from the content management system software which this book will focus on (although much of the information in this book will still be relevant).

Who is this book for?

You know what a blog is, but you certainly don't want all the technical details of how a plugin works.

You have some computer skills and you have just been put in charge of managing a WordPress website. That is who this book for – someone who may not be a web developer, who needs to manage and maintain a WordPress website.

For example...

- Perhaps someone has created a website for you and you now need to learn how to manage and update it.

- You are a marketing manager who needs to update content on your website.

- You may have started a new job that involves updating your employer's website.

- Or the web person at your work has left and the responsibility has now fallen onto you to manage your company's web presence!

You are less interested in building a new website, and more interested in managing existing ones!

If you are a web developer who wants to learn advanced topics on customising WordPress installations, creating plugins and themes from scratch - this book is not for you!

This book is for anyone who wants to know how to keep their website up-to-date, and want to know the essentials for the day-to-day management of their WordPress website.

You won't find advanced theory or information about coding in this book – just the facts and an introduction on how to manage the different aspects of your website.

Perhaps you use desktop applications (e.g. Microsoft Word) and you know how to turn on a computer – but you may not be familiar with WordPress, content management systems or creating websites.

What this book covers

There are many books covering WordPress that go extensively into technical detail, covering installation, customising themes and other advanced topics. These books are perfect for someone wanting to create a WordPress website from scratch (e.g. a web developer) – but not so great for someone who just wants to update their website!

While this book will touch very briefly on some of these subjects, it will primarily focus on managing an existing WordPress website.

This book covers editing pages, keeping WordPress updated and other routine tasks that may be required of someone managing and updating a WordPress website. This book is aimed as an introduction rather then a comprehensive guide to each and every aspect of WordPress.

You can either read this book page by page to learn how to manage your website, or have it by your computer and use as a reference. Hopefully this will provide you enough skills and a starting point to find further information when required.

WordPress Features

WordPress includes many features, including...

- **Plugins** – used to extend the functionality of your website, for example including file uploads, social media integration, customised logins, etc. If WordPress does not have a feature you require, chances are you will be able to add it using a plugin.

- **Users** – you can manage who can add, edit and make changes to your website, and whether visitors can register and post stuff. There are different levels of users, including administrators (who can do pretty much anything) and subscribers (who have more restricted access) – in some cases there may only be one user (the person responsible for managing the website) depending on the nature of the website.

- **Themes** – many themes are available for changing the layout and appearance of your website, and you can customise themes yourself to give your website a unique look.

- **Blogs** – WordPress includes features for blogging, which is also ideal for a news section of the website, although this can be disabled if you are not interested in a blog/news section.

These features are covered in greater detail within their own chapters.

Installing and setting up WordPress

While this book focuses on managing a WordPress website after installation, this section will provide a very brief overview to obtaining, installing and setting up WordPress.

Hosting your website

Before you begin, ensure your hosting supports WordPress. Some specifically say they support WordPress, and some even offer to install WordPress (although this may be a cut-down version).

A full list of hosting requirements is available from the WordPress website. As a guide WordPress requires the following on your web hosting or server:

- PHP
- MySQL
- Apache web server (you may also wish to install the **mod_rewrite** module for Apache to give your web addresses clearer names)

Most hosting (particularly using Linux hosting) will have these installed as standard, however check the versions installed compared to the versions WordPress currently supports. If in doubt, e-mail the web hosting company and ask!

Obtaining & Installing WordPress

You can download the files for WordPress from **www.wordpress.org** – on the home page is a link to download the latest version of WordPress.

1) Unzip the file that you have downloaded, you can do this from Windows by double clicking the file then copying the contents to another folder.

2) Create a database in MySQL for WordPress – your hosting provider will usually allow you to do this from their Control Panel or provide you with information on how to do this.

3) Upload the files that you unzipped to your hosting.

4) With a web browser (e.g. Internet Explorer or Google Chrome) go to: **www.websitename.co.uk/wp-admin/install.php** – where **websitename.co.uk** is the web address for your website, and then follow the steps to install WordPress.

Customising themes and tailoring the look of your WordPress website is beyond the scope of this book. However you may wish to check the dashboard settings and customise the website, themes, etc. - including changing the permalinks option in **Settings** to ensure your web addresses look more friendlier. And remember to check your website is up and running – ideally on different computers/web browsers.

Introducing The Dashboard

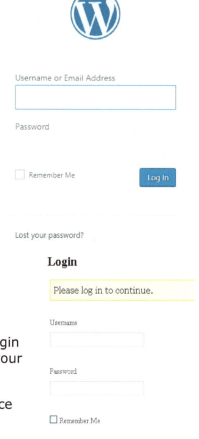

The Dashboard is your "control panel" where you manage your website, for example editing pages and managing users.

Administrators have full access to the dashboard, while other types of users may only have limited access to change their own details (and you can disable access to the dashboard for non administrators) or post content.

To log in, enter your username and password – you should see a login link or form somewhere on your website. If not, check with the person who set up the website, or try typing the following web address:

www.websitename.co.uk/wp-admin
(Replace **websitename.co.uk** with the address of your website.)

This hopefully takes you to a login page where you can log in to your dashboard.

The login page may have the appearance of the standard WordPress login page (see first illustration) or you may have a plugin installed to give your login page the same appearance as the rest of your website.

If you share your computer with other people, remember to log out once you have finished!

Your username & password

Hopefully you obtained your username and password from your web developer/designer.

You can also use the e-mail address associated with your account as your username (and if you forget or don't have your username try entering your e-mail address).

If you forget or don't know your password, reset your password using the **Lost Password** link.

Navigating the dashboard

At the left-hand side are links to different sections. Some plugins add their own items to this navigation bar, e.g. if you installed a visitor tracking plugin (alternatively the plugin may place a link to their section under the **Tools** or **Settings** sections).

Place your mouse pointer over an item to see sub-items, or click an item go to that items main section (the sub-items then appear underneath).

Some items may have a number beside them with a red circle – this indicates there are updates available (e.g. new versions of the WordPress software and updated versions of plugins) – you can go to the appropriate section and then select whether to install the updates.

Each item is covered in greater detail in their own chapters.

Toolbar

When logged in, you will see this toolbar at the top of the dashboard and website:

Options vary depending on how your website is set up, plugins you are using and your access to the website (e.g. "Subscriber" will see less sections then administrators). This includes:

 The WordPress logo in the far corner includes options to take you to the WordPress website (**www.wordpress.org**) and displaying help, support and documentation.

 Your website name includes an option to take you to your main website (although you will still be logged in) – when you are in the main part of your website you will see options to go to the various sections of the dashboard.

 How many updates are available for WordPress and installed items (plugins / themes / etc.). Click to view a list of available updates and then optionally install them.

 Links to add new users, pages, blog posts and other items.

 In the right-hand corner are options to log out and amend your details (including password and profile picture).

You can hide the toolbar, or hide the toolbar for particular users, by installing a plugin. Go to the install plugins part of the dashboard and search for "hide toolbar".

Editing Pages & Content

Pages. Pretty much every website has them!

Different pages can provide different types of information, for example about who you or your company are, your products/services, etc.

Every time a visitor clicks a navigation link and goes to a different part of your website, they are going to a different page. In some cases they may go to the blog (if that is set up) or a login page, but otherwise they are visiting a WordPress page.

Apart from blog posts, pages are probably the item you will edit and make changes to the most on your website.

To view settings and details for the pages on your website, and to add/edit existing pages, go to the **Pages** section on the dashboard.

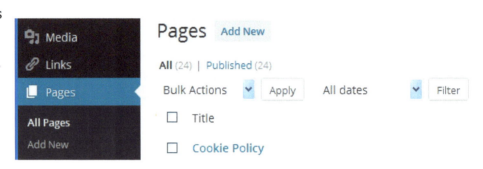

Editing an existing page

In the **Pages** section of the WordPress dashboard, click the **Edit** link or page name to edit that page. Alternatively you may see an Edit link on each page of your website when you are logged in.

You can edit a page just as you would edit a document in Microsoft Word, with different formatting options, options to add pictures, etc.

Recent versions of WordPress introduce a new editor – known as the Blocks editor – which is different to the editor previously used in WordPress. With the new editor you don't see the toolbar at the top – instead you type in text, and then select the text to format that block of text, e.g. setting font size, etc.

If you don't like the Blocks editor, and would prefer to use the classic style editor, there are plugins available that provide the classic editor.

At the top you can change the title of the page (this change may be reflected in any navigation links).

In the editor section, you format your text just as you would in a word processor, for example making text bold, adding bullet points/numbering, etc.

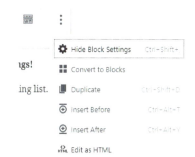

With the Blocks editor (or if you can't see the top toolbar), select the text to see the formatting options.

Editing HTML

Usually you will edit the page using a **visual** style – just like editing a document in Microsoft Word or another application – i.e. it will be as it appears on the page, with any formatting, etc.

If you have problems editing the page visually, or prefer to edit the HTML, select the button at the top, to the right of the editor (with the three dots) and from the menu select **Edit as HTML**.

Adding a web link

To add a link to another page, another website or an e-mail address, select the text and click the icon that has the appearance of a chain joined together. You can also use this button to change an existing web link (by selecting the web link and clicking the button).

A small box will then appear below the text – from here you can either type in (or copy and paste) the web address to link to. Then click the blue button or press enter to apply.

To cancel, just click anywhere outside the link options.

To link to another page or existing content, click the cog button on the right: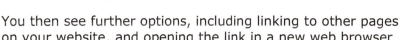

You then see further options, including linking to other pages on your website, and opening the link in a new web browser tab. Click the **Add Link** button to apply the link.

Clicking the button with the broken chain removes the web link (although the text will remain).

After adding a web link and editing the page – remember to go to the page on your website and test the web link! Make sure it works as expected – you don't want your visitors to discover the web link does not work!

Adding an image to the page

 To add an image to the page, click the **Add Media** button in the classic editor, that appears just above the editor and formatting options.

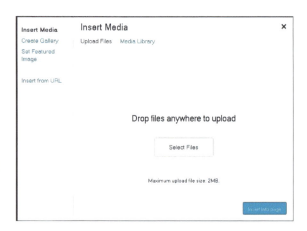

From the box that appears, you can upload a file from your computer.

Alternatively, select the **Media Library** tab to add an image already on your website (e.g. on another page/post).

Click the **Insert into page** button to add the image to the page. Cancel adding an image by clicking the small cross that appears in the top right-hand corner.

If you are using the Blocks editor, or can't see the option, click the **Add Image** button which appears next to your current location in the editor – you will then be presented with options to upload an image, add an image from your media library, etc.:

Page attributes and options

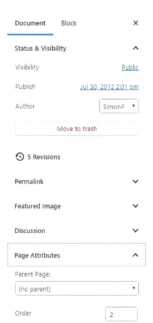

On the right-hand side you can see options for your page – select the **Document** tab at the top if you can't see them.

To see a particular set of options that are hidden, click the section titles (e.g. clicking "Page Attributes" will reveal the page attributes options).

The **Page Attributes** section sets the following two options, which mainly effect how links to the page will appear in any navigation links:

- **Parent** – set the page up as a sub-section of another page. If a page has a parent, the link to that page appears as a menu or sub-section in any navigation bar or link.

- **Order** – where the page will appear in any navigation links, otherwise pages are sorted alphabetically. Pages with a lower number appear first, for example when one page has the order number of "1" and then another page the order number of "2", page "1" will appear first in any navigation menu.

You may wish to explore some of the other options, e.g. the permalink option, featured images and discussions/comments.

Previewing & saving changes

You can preview how the page will look (i.e. how a visitor to your website will see it) before saving any changes by clicking the **Preview** button at the top right.

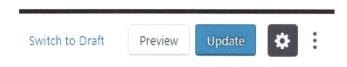

Click the **Update** button at the right-hand side to apply changes you have made to the page.

Adding a new page

In the Pages section of the dashboard, click the **Add New** button at the top to add a new page.

Depending on how your website is set up, the page may not automatically appear in navigation bars, sections, etc. so you may also need to edit the navigation settings of your website (you can usually edit the navigation bar from your theme's settings or the **Appearance** / **Widgets** dashboard section).

You can set the page title, and add content to your page.

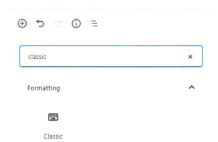

Click the **Publish** button to save and publish the new page.

New pages will use the new Blocks editor by default – if you'd rather use the classic editor, you can either install a plugin, or click the "Add Block" button at the top right, in the search box type in "Classic" and then select the Classic option that appears – this will insert a classic style editor into your page.

For more on the editing options, see "Editing an existing page".

Deleting a page

To delete a page, go to the **Pages** section of the dashboard, and put your mouse pointer over the row with the page you wish to delete. Click the **Trash** link that appears to delete the page.

You may need to edit your navigation bars after deleting a page, to ensure none of the navigation bars contain links to the deleted page. You will also need to ensure any other links to that page are updated.

If you wish to hide the page from visitors, instead of deleting you may wish to edit the page and set the **Visibility** (within the **Publish** options) to **Private**.

Blogs

WordPress was originally created as a blogging platform, and while including a blog on your website is optional, it is still a key and very useful feature.

If you have multiple people managing your website, you can allow them to post to your blog, or you may wish to create user accounts for different members of staff to post blogs.

You can use your website's blog as a news section for your website, for example keeping visitors up-to-date with what is happening within your company.

To manage your website's blogs, go to the **Posts** section of the dashboard.

Posting a blog

From the Posts section of the dashboard, select **Add New**.

In many ways, posting a blog is just like adding/editing a page, or documents in another application (e.g. Microsoft Word).

As with pages, recent versions of WordPress start using the Blocks editor.

Type in the title of your post and its content. There are various formatting options, and you can add pictures, links, etc.

You can preview the blog post, and also assign different categories. For example, you might have categories for different types of news items, etc.

For further information on editing and various formatting options, see the "Editing an existing page" and "Adding a new page" sections of the "Pages" chapter of this book.

Managing comments

Depending on how you have set up your website and blog, visitors may be able to post comments.

You can set up your blog so only those who have registered can post comments, and for comments to be approved before they become visible on the website.

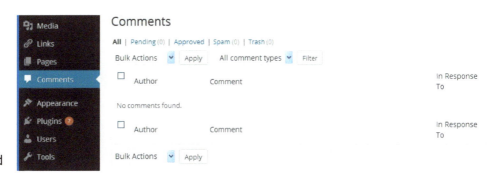

You usually receive an e-mail when someone posts a comment. If you begin having issues with comments that are spam, you can delete those comments, and perhaps change the settings so you can approve comments before they are posted.

To manage comments, go to the **Comments** section of the dashboard.

Approving comments

When comments are set up so approval is required, it is up to you to determine whether to allow them to be posted, and if its a company website you may have policies and rules for this.

To change settings for comments (e.g. to change the way comments are posted so approval is required before comments become publicly visible) go to the **Settings** section of the dashboard, and then to **Discussion**.

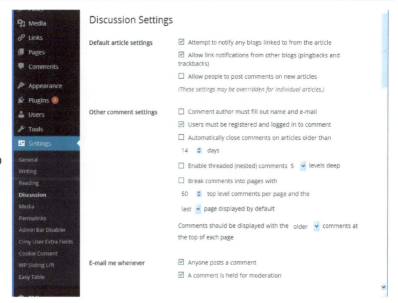

Managing blog posts

From the **Posts** section of the dashboard, you can edit existing blog posts, change the different categories and delete blog posts.

Place your mouse pointer over the blog post to see the options to edit and delete (by clicking the **Trash** link) the post.

Orkney Night

Edit | Quick Edit | Trash | View

You can also view and manage comments for that blog post.

From the **Posts** section of the dashboard you can see the author of the blog post and any categories. If you click a category, the list will only display blog posts with that author/category.

gordongetbirli
n

Events, Uncategorized

Allowing multiple users to blog

You can allow other users on your website to add blog posts, for example different people within your company may wish to blog about their area of expertise.

You can let other people to blog without giving them full administrative access to the website.

Role

First Name

From the **Users** section of the Dashboard, select the user you want to allow to blog, and change their access from "Subscriber" to "Author" or "Contributor". If the user has administrative access then don't change anything, as they can already blog on your website, and changing it will reduce what they have access to!

For further information, see the "Managing Users" chapter of this book.

Managing Users

WordPress websites can have multiple users.

These can be people registered on your website or you have added and set up yourself.

For example, you may set up additional users to assist with managing the website or allow visitors to register to access additional content.

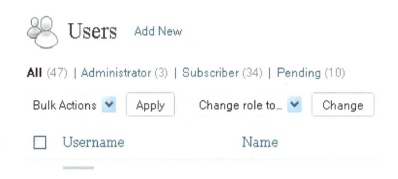

You can have different levels of users, from **Administrators** who can pretty much do anything to **Subscribers** who can access additional content but not make any changes.

There will be at least one user – the person responsible for administrating and managing the website – presumably you since you are reading this book!

Website Users

Encourage users of your website to change their password after they have signed in for the first time. They should not share their password with anyone else – not even you!

Try to keep usernames in a consistent format to make the website easier to manage, for example...

- Setting the usernames to the member's full name (e.g. "**Joe Bloggs**")

- Using the first initial and last name (e.g. "**jbloggs**")

This will help make managing users much easier!

Adding new users

To add a new user, go to the **Users** section of the dashboard and select **Add New** – you will find this option in the sidebar and at the top of the section.

From the **Add New User** page you can enter the details for the new user, for example their username, e-mail address and full name. You can also enter the address for their website if they have one.

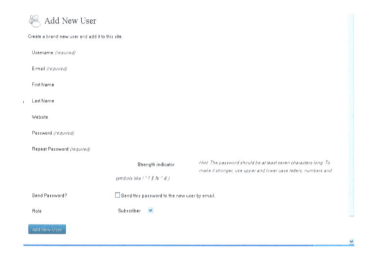

You can enter an initial password for the user, and will be advised of the password strength (the stronger the password the less likely someone can guess what the password is).

Tick the **Send this password to the new user by e-mail** option to have the username and password e-mailed to the new user.

Finally, you can set the **Role** for the user – "Subscriber" is the most basic type of user account, and will not have administrative access to your website. Other roles, e.g. "Administrator" have more access to the website, can make changes, etc.

Click the **Add New User** button to add the new user to the website.

Deleting users

You may wish to delete a user from the website, for example if they misbehave, or they no longer work for your organisation.

You can delete a user account by going to the **Users** section of the dashboard and clicking the **Delete** link for that user.

Remember that when you delete a user, this action can not be undone – if you wish to reinstate that user you will have to create a new user account for them!

Approving new users

If you allow visitors to your website to register, you may have it set up so that you approve new users before they are allowed to log in. You will usually receive an e-mail alerting you of any new users.

To approve a new user, go to the **Users** section of the dashboard. For the new user, you will notice their role is "Pending".

Click the **Approve** link that appears when you put your mouse pointer over the users name to approve their user account, and allow them to log into the website.

If you wish to decline their request to join the website, click **Delete**.

You can also click the users name to edit/view their profile details, which may help you in making a decision whether to approve their membership. You can approve their access by editing the **Role** field from "Pending" to "Subscriber".

The user will receive an e-mail when you approve their user account.

Editing existing users

To edit the details for an existing user, select the **Edit** link for that user or click their name.

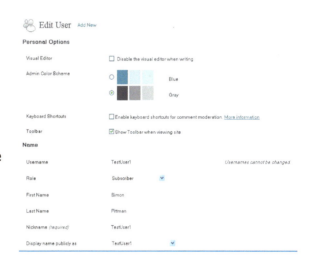

You will then be able change their details from the page that appears, for example their role/access to the website, e-mail address and password.

When a user edits their own details (for example to change their password) they see a similar page.

This is very similar to the page for adding a new user, or registering on your website.

Your user account

To edit details for your own profile (e.g. your e-mail address or changing your password) go to the **Users** section of the dashboard, and select **Your Profile**.

User roles

You can assign different levels of access to different members, for example administrators have overall control of the website, while subscribers have access to particular content and features but can not make any changes to the website itself.

From the **Users** section of the dashboard you can see which roles users have, at the top of the list are links to view only members with a particular role.

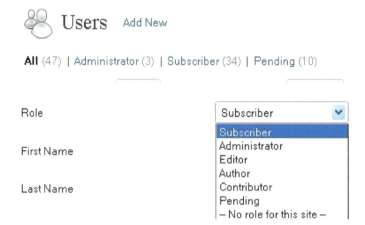

To change a users role, click the username to view their profile, and change their role.

The roles available include...

- **Administrator** – these users can make any changes to the website, add/delete users, etc.

- **Subscriber** – this is usually the default role assigned to new users, very basic access to read and access content.

- **Pending** – assigned to new user accounts where administrator's approval is required first. An administrator can approve the account, usually by changing the role to Subscriber. Pending users can not log into the website until their user account is approved.

- **Editor** – this role can post content and make changes to other people's content. Particularly useful if you wish for someone to assist you with managing the website, but not provide them full administrative access.

- **Author** – these users can post and make changes to their own content. This role would be useful if you wish for people within your company to write a blog, news items, etc. The **Contributor** role is similar, but with this role posts can not be published.

If you are unsure what role a user should be given, then you may wish to give them **Subscriber** access initially.

Be careful who you give **Administrator** access to – they have complete control over users, website content, etc. - they could even delete you from the website!

The number of administrator users can vary, but it is best to avoid having too many – aim for 2 or 3 at most. Only provide administrator access to people you trust, who need administrative access and who will be helping with your website! As an alternative, you can give someone helping you manage the website the **Editor** role.

Backing up your website

Backing up your website is very important – if anything happens with your hosting or files, you could lose your entire website and content!

Your web hosting company will usually create backups of their servers, or if your website is hosted on your own server then your IT department may make regular backups. However you may still wish to create your own backups.

Backing up files by copying the files from your hosting to your computer will not work, as this will not back up the database used by WordPress.

The standard installation of WordPress does not provide a way of creating or automating backups of your website, so you will either have to use your own backup software, or install a plugin for backing up your website.

Who is currently backing up your website?

Are backups currently being created?

Check and find out how, when and if your website is being backed up.

How often to create backups

This can depend on how often content on your website is changed – if you only update your website once a month there is little point in creating weekly backups for example! Likewise if you have users registering and active, content updated, etc. on a daily basis, then more regular backups should be created (possibly on a daily basis).

Use your judgement and decide how often to back up, and make sure you get in the habit of creating the backups, or find a plugin to automate this.

The most important thing is that you create backups on a regular basis.

You may wish to create a schedule/checklist of the dates you will back up your website, look for tools to automate backing up your website (remember to check regularly that the backups are actually created if you do this!) or set up reminders on your computer, to ensure you remember to back up your website.

Plugins for backing up website

There are plugins available for backing up your website – including plugins that will create a complete backup of your website that you can then download.

Search for "website backup" when adding a new plugin (see the "Plugins" chapter of this book for further details on plugins and how to install them).

When backing up your website, you may wish to do it during the night or early morning, or at another time when there is very little traffic on your website. While you are backing up your website using a plugin, it may slow down the website for visitors, and it will ensure that backups are not disrupted.

Further information on backups

If you would like further information on backing up a WordPress website, you can read the documentation on the WordPress website, available at:

https://wordpress.org/support/article/wordpress-backups/

This includes a list of plugins available for creating backups, in addition to instructions on backing up your website and database manually.

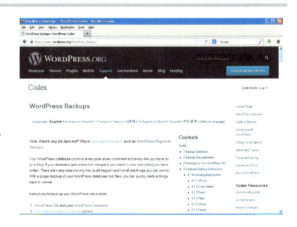

Installing Updates

The dashboard indicates when there are updates available for WordPress and any installed plugins and themes, both in the right-hand corner of the main dashboard section and in the top bar – when there are updates the number of available updates will be displayed.

Click either of these to see a list of updates available - you then have options to install them.

Before installing updates, you may wish to consider backing up your website, especially when installing major updates, e.g. updating the main WordPress software.

The updates page will advise you if there is a newer version of WordPress available. Click the **Update Now** button to install the new version of WordPress.

You may wish to carry out this update at a time when disruption to visitors is minimal.

On the page is a list of updates for plugins, and you can select which plugins you wish to update and click the **Update Plugins** button to install the updates.

Similarly you may see a list of updates for themes you have installed. You can select which updates you wish to install then click the **Update Themes** button. Be aware that updating themes may make changes to the appearance of your website, although this will be less of an issue if you use child themes (a modified version of an existing theme).

Media & Uploading Files

The Media section of the dashboard contains any images and other files that have been added to your website.

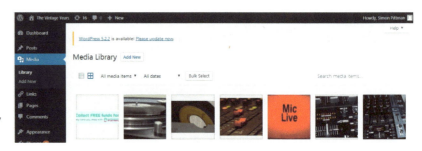

When editing a page or blog post, any photos you add will automatically be added to the Media section – you can then use the photo in other parts of your website (e.g. other pages/posts).

You can also upload items directly by clicking **Add New link**:

For example, you may wish to include files for your visitors to download (e.g. a Word or PDF document), photos/videos used in other parts of your website (e.g. within the navigation bar of your website), etc.

Click an item to view options to edit that items details, delete the item or view/download the item. If you wish to edit the file's actual contents, you will need to download the file, edit it on your computer and add that item again.

From the top of your media, you can select how you view your items – e.g. a grid, or a list of items:

When editing a page or blog post, to include an item from the media library:

In the classic editor, click the **Add Media** button to add an item to your page.

In the Blocks editor (or if you don't see the classic editor buttons) click the **Add Image** button to the right, and then select **Media Library**.

Links to other websites

Your website may include a bar with links to other websites, e.g. near the navigation bar, which is visible regardless of which page you go to.

These can be edited from the **Links** section of the dashboard.

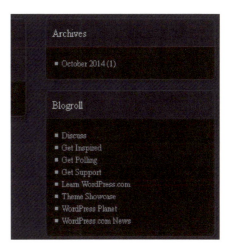

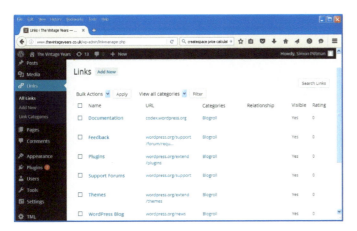

If a page includes links to other websites, or you have a page dedicated to web links, then you can edit those web links by editing the page that contains the web links.

To edit the web links details, put your mouse pointer over that web link and select **Edit**. To remove that web link, click **Delete**.

To add a new web link, click the **Add New** button.

Plugins

Plugins help you to extend the functionality of your website by adding new features that may not be included in the standard WordPress installation, for example you might install plugins to...

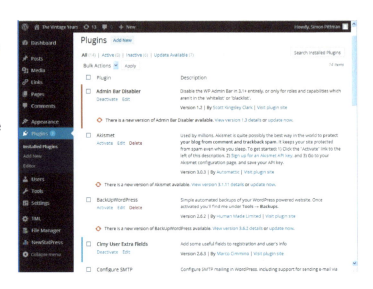

- Display a notice on your website on the use of cookies, ensuring compliance to EU cookie regulations.

- Customise or extend logins and registrations to the website.

- Track visitors to your website.

- Add a contact form.

- Back up your website.

To view a list of plugins currently installed on your website, go to the **Plugins** section of the dashboard. From this section you can change settings for installed plugins, update to newer versions and disable plugins you do not require.

At the top are links to only view a list of active (currently in use), inactive (plugins you have disabled) and plugins where newer versions are available.

Updating Plugins

The list of plugins will indicate if there is a newer version of that plugin available – you can view details of the update or click the **Update now** link for that plugin to update to the new version.

Updates can not only contain new features for that plugin, but also bug fixes and fixing any security issues from previous versions. Read the information for the update carefully before installing the update, and if in doubt speak to your web developer.

After installing an update, check your website (particularly any pages that use the plugin) to make sure everything is still working, and that the update hasn't broken anything!

Installing Plugins

Only install a plugin to fulfil a requirement – and not just for the sake of installing that particular plugin! Consider what tasks or functions you require from your website, and if its not provided by WordPress or any of the currently installed plugins, then look for a plugin to fulfil your requirement. Don't just browse the plugins for things that "sound cool"!

Unless you wish to add an additional functionality to your website, you should not need to install any new plugins if the website has been set up for you – and you may wish to speak to your web developer before making any changes.

To install a new plugin, go to the **Plugins** section of the dashboard.

Click the **Add new** link at the top Plugins section, or the link in the navigation bar.

To search for a plugin from the page that appears type in what you are looking for (for example if you are looking for a plugin to display a reminder about cookies, you could type in "cookie reminder") then press enter or click the **Search Plugins** button.

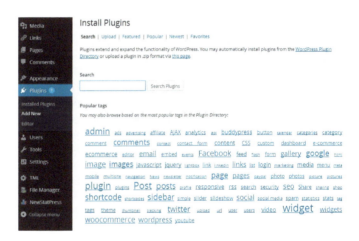

You can also click on one of the words in the **Popular tags** area to search for that item.

At the top of the page are options to upload a plugin you may have on your computer, or to view the most popular or newest plugins.

From the list that appears, you can browse the matching plugins that have been found.

The **Ratings** column gives you an idea how useful other WordPress users have found that particular plugin.

Click the **Details** link below the plugin name to view further details for that plugin, including a detailed description, link to the developers website, screenshots of how the plugin will appear and installation information. There are links at the top of the plugin information to take you to the different information available.

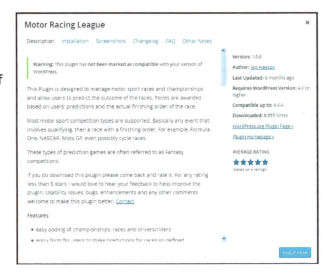

To install a plugin, click the **Install Now** button on the plugins details page, or the **Install Now** link below the plugin name.

Choosing the right plugin

Before you begin looking for a plugin, be aware that while many plugins are available free of charge, some plugins may require a payment, or have a free version that displays advertising. Check the documentation, terms and conditions and price of any plugin before installing.

When choosing a plugin for a particular task, consider and look at the following...

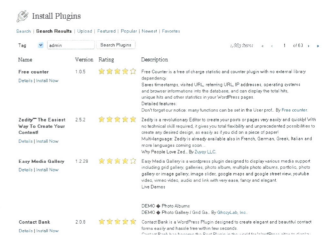

- Read the reviews for the plugin.

- Check when the plugin was last updated and if it is compatible with the version of WordPress you are using.

- Is the plugin available free of charge, is it free with certain restrictions, etc.?

- Will the plugin interfere with any other plugins installed?

- Do you really need the plugin? What purpose/task will the plugin fulfil?

Managing plugins

From the **Plugins** section of the dashboard you will see a list of installed plugins, and from here you can uninstall, update or disable them.

If you want to disable a plugin, click the **Deactivate** link underneath the plugin name. While the plugin will still be installed, it will not be in use by your website. To enable an inactive plugin, select **Activate**.

☐ **Admin Bar Disabler**
Deactivate | Edit

You can also completely remove the plugin. Click the red **Delete** link for a plugin to uninstall. When you remove a plugin, any settings for that plugin will also be lost.

☐ **Akismet**
Activate | Edit | Delete

For some plugins, you will see a **Settings** link that lets you change settings particular to that plugin.

☐ **WP Sliding Login | Register Panel**
Settings | Deactivate | Edit

For more advanced users, the **Edit** option allows you to make changes to the plugins code and modify how it works – however be warned that editing the plugin this way may stop the plugin from working correctly if you do not know what you are doing!

While sometimes it may be tempting to install as many plugins as possible, it is best to avoid getting carried away with too many plugins. Too many plugins could potentially slow down your website!

Disable or uninstall any plugins that you do not use or are not required – you could disable a plugin that is not being used initially, and if you still do not use it after a while you could completely uninstall it. Remember that you can install a plugin again in the future if you delete it, but later find that you do require it after all.

If a plugin is causing your website or other plugins to behave strangely or in an unexpected manner, then disable or uninstall that plugin. This could happen if you have more then one plugin carrying out similar tasks.

WordPress alerts you when there are updates and new versions available, and you will have the option of installing the updated plugin.

☐ **Theme My Login**
Deactivate | Edit

Themes the WordPress login, registration and forgot password p

Version 6.3.8 | By Jeff Farthing | Visit plugin site

There is a new version of Theme My Login available. View version 6.3.9 details or update now.

Settings for individual plugins

Some plugins have their own section and settings within the WordPress dashboard.

A link for changing settings for particular plugins can sometimes be found within the **Plugins** section of the dashboard, within the list of installed plugins.

WP Slidi
Settings | [

Alternatively you may find the plugin settings within the **Settings** section of the dashboard, as sub-items of that section.

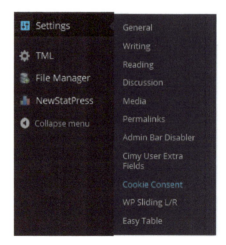

You can then change and adjust settings for these plugins. It is worth checking and where appropriate changing the settings after installing or updating a plugin.

If you can not find any settings for the plugin, then it may not be possible to change settings for that plugin.

Themes

Themes allow you to change and alter the look of your website – there are many themes available created by other people, and you can create your own themes and modify and tailor existing ones to your needs.

To change settings for your themes, go to the **Appearance** section of the dashboard.

From the **Appearance** section you can also edit navigation bars, sidebars and other design elements on your website.

Your web designer will probably have already set up the theme, design and layout for your website. As this book is aimed at those responsible for managing an existing website, themes will only be covered in very brief detail.

Finding and installing themes

Many themes available free of charge – however be aware that some themes may require payment or come with their own terms and conditions (for example free only for personal use) – check the documentation for each theme before installing.

To install a new theme, select **Install Themes** from the **Appearance** and **Themes** section of the dashboard.

You can then search for keywords, or select features you wish to be included in a theme. Click the **Find Themes** button to see a list of matching themes.

At the top you can see options to upload your own theme, or view "featured", recently updated or newly available themes.

When browsing the list of themes, put your mouse pointer over the theme to see options for that theme - click the **Preview** link to see how the theme will appear on your website, or select **Install** to install the theme.

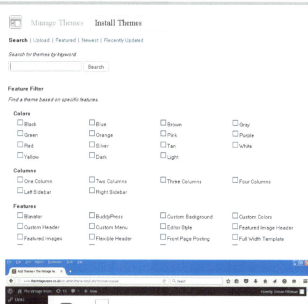

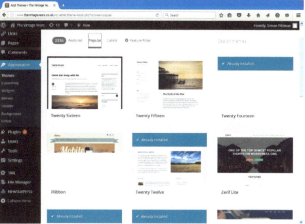

Setting up themes

To apply a theme to your website, select the **Activate** link in the list of themes (this will appear when you put your mouse pointer over a theme). You can also preview the theme to see how it will appear with your website using the **Live Preview** option.

The **Customize** link for a theme allows you to make changes to colours, header images, etc.

If you wish to make more extensive changes, you could create a child theme.

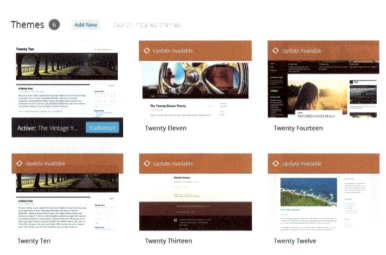

Altering themes/child themes

If you modify a theme, you may wish to instead create a "Child Theme", which uses an existing theme as a template, but only holds the changes/features you have made for the theme.

Any changes made to the theme will not be lost when you update the parent theme.

For example, while a theme may be suitable for your needs, you may wish to customise how it appears to match any other materials, colours, etc. used by your company.

☐ **One-Click Child Theme**
Activate | Edit | Delete

Allows you to easily child theme any theme from the theme

Version 1.2 | By tychay | Visit plugin site

Unfortunately WordPress does not have a method for automatically creating a child theme, so you may wish to install a plugin to assist with this, for example "One Click Child Theme". Once this plugin in installed, you will see an option in the list of themes to create a child theme.

Modifying and creating new themes is beyond the aims of this book.

WordPress Settings

From the Settings section of the dashboard you can manage and set overall settings for your website. Chances are you will very rarely need to change settings once your website is set up.

In addition to the settings mentioned here, you may also see additional sections and settings for some of the plugins you have installed.

General Settings

From here you can set up information including the name of your website, domain name, a contact e-mail address, whether visitors to the website can register for a user account, and time zones/formats.

It is unlikely you will need to change these settings for your website.

When making changes to any of the categories, remember to click the **Save Changes** button at the bottom of the page for the changes to take effect!

Writing Settings

These settings relate to writing blogs.

For example, setting default categories for blogs and posting by e-mail.

Reading Settings

These set whether the home page (the first page a visitor to your website sees) displays the blog or one of the pages.

You can also set the number of blog posts displayed per page, and whether to discourage search engines from finding your website (which is something you probably don't want to do!).

Discussion Settings

From here, you can change settings related to comments that visitors can post on your website – and whether they can even post them!

If you have problems with spam comments being posted, you can review these settings.

Settings that may be of interest include...

- **Comment author must fill out name and e-mail** – particularly useful when members of the public can post comments, and can help discourage spam/abusive comments.

- **Users must be registered and logged in to comment** – with this enabled, if a visitor to your website does not have a user account and are not logged in, they can not comment on posts and pages. If you have this option enabled, you will not need to have the above option (filling out name/e-mail) enabled.

- **Automatically close comments on articles older then...** - with this option enabled, anything older then the number of days specified can not have comments posted – also useful for cutting down on spam.

If you have problems with spam or abusive/heated discussions you could enable the **Comment must be manually approved** option. If you also select the options to receive e-mails when a **Comment is held for moderation** you will receive an e-mail when there are comments requiring your approval.

You can also have comments requiring your approval if it contains a specific number of web links, or particular words.

The final set of options within this section are for **Avatars**, pictures that can appear beside comments, for example if it is a registered user it may display a photo of that user beside the comment.

Media Settings

These are settings for images that are posted, particularly the size of the images and how they are organised.

Permalinks Settings

This ensures that the web address for each page looks friendly and makes sense, e.g.

www.mywebsite.com/pagename rather then **www.mywebsite.com/?p=321**

From here, you can set how web addresses are formatted (and therefore how they appear in the address bar).

Usually, you will want to set this option to be **Post Name** – however you may have a different preference.

Frequently Asked Questions

General Usage

I can't find the link to login on my website!

If your website is designed to only allow you (and other people responsible for managing content) to login, rather then members of the public, the login link may be hidden. Try one of the following:

- Check for a link to login at the bottom of your website, this could be called "Login", "Admin" or similar.

- Type in the following web address: **www.mywebsite.co.uk/wp-admin/** (replacing **www.mywebsite.co.uk** with the web address for your website)

- Similarly, try **www.mywebsite.co.uk/wp-login.php** (again replacing **www.mywebsite.co.uk** with your web address)

Can I use photos, images and content from other websites on my own website?
Can I use photos I find in Google Images search results?

Content from other websites will be copyrighted – never use content or photos from other websites, Google searches, etc. without permission from the copyright owner/author of that work – imagine how you would feel if someone took content from your website!

Only use photos and content that you have created yourself, or you have permission to use.

You may wish to look for a website that provides stock photographs or public domain images, however you may have to pay to use the photos, and check the copyright carefully.

I've forgotten my password – can I reset it?

- If there is another user with administrator access, ask them to change your password – they can enter a new password by changing your profile details in the **Users** section of the dashboard.

- You may see a "Lost Password" link below the login form, click this and enter your details to receive a new password.

My website looks different on different web browsers – how can I fix this?

- Check to see if there is an updated version of the theme you are using.

- Investigate using another theme that has better support for the different web browsers.

Do I need a user account on WordPress.com to manage my WordPress website?

No – WordPress.com is completely separate from the WordPress software you use. You only need a user account on your own website!

Do visitors need a user account to access my website?

No. You can restrict some content so that only registered users can see it.

Can I add links to other websites?

- You can add links to other websites on any of the pages.

- There may be a list of links on your website (e.g. at the side) similar to the navigation links, etc. that you can edit from the **Links** section of the dashboard.

- You may wish to check with the owner of the website before adding a link to them.

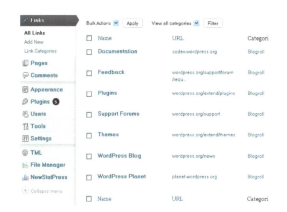

Can I customise what navigation bars appear on my website and where?

Go to the **Appearance** section of the dashboard and then **Widgets**. From here you can add and change navigation bars, login links, and any other items you wish to appear on your website.

The number of widgets you can have on your website and the layout can vary depending on which theme you are using.

Administration & Management

When I post, how can I ensure that non-admin users only see what I want them to see?

The easiest way is to create a non-administrative user account for yourself (e.g. **TestUser**) with "Subscriber" permissions (or whichever role you wish to test). Log in using this user account to check that users can only see and have access to what you want them to see!

Can I customise the e-mail that is sent to new users, etc.?

Yes, install a plugins for this - e.g. when installing a new plugin search for "theme my login" which not only lets you customise e-mails sent to new users but also content of e-mails they receive, etc.

☐ **Theme My Login**
Deactivate | Edit

Themes the WordPress login, registration and for

Version 6.3.8 | By Jeff Farthing | Visit plugin site

How can I track the number of visitors to my website?

Your web hosting may provide statistics on visitors to your website, and you can also install plugins to assist with this (search for "visitor statistics" when installing a plugin).

Username

Password

How do I remove the standard WordPress login so it has the same look as the rest of my website?

There are plugins that can help with this – e.g. go to the **Plugins** section of the dashboard, and add a new plugin, searching for "Theme My Login".

☐ Remember Me

Log In

Do I need to let visitors to my website know that my website uses cookies?

If you need to advise visitors that your website uses cookies (e.g. to comply with EU regulations) various plugins are available for this – search for "cookie warning" plugins and then look at which plugin is best for your website.

How do I remove the WordPress bar at the top of the website, so people can't see it when they are logged in?

Install a plugin for this task, e.g. search for "Admin Bar Disabler" or "Disable toolbar" in the **Plugins** section when installing a new plugin.

Will visitors to my website know that I am using WordPress?

It won't be obvious to visitors that you use WordPress. While some themes include the WordPress logo, or a "Created using WordPress" text somewhere, these can be removed and hidden.

Can I add a contact form to my website?

Yes – you can install and set up a plugin that will allow you to add a contact form.

My website is not secure (it doesn't display HTTPS or have the padlock symbol in the titlebar) – how do I fix this?

This is not something that can be fixed from within WordPress – contact your web hosting as they will be able to fix this for you.

Can I prevent spam comments?

Go to the **Settings** section of the dashboard, and then go to **Discussion** - from here you can change settings for comments, e.g. so only registered users can post comments and an administrator needs to approve any comments.

You can also install a plugin to help prevent comment spam, for example a plugin that requires a "captcha" code to be entered before a comment is submitted.

What do I need to do to ensure my website is GDPR compliant?

- Review and update your website's privacy policy (or create one if it doesn't already exist) – including information on how visitor's data is used.

- Display a notification on your website that the website uses cookies.

- On any sign-up/registration forms, include information on how you will use your visitors data. Make sure you are only keeping data on visitors/customers that you need to keep, the data is secure and that you have a reason for keeping data about them.

- You will probably find a lot of the above already exists, or only needs slight tweaks. You may also wish to seek further help, either legally, from a trade body or from the government's website.

Getting further help and information

Help within WordPress

At the top right-hand corner of the dashboard you will see a **Help** button which will display additional information, and also take you to more detailed documentation.

WordPress Website & Documentation

There is a range of documentation available from the WordPress website:

codex.wordpress.org

This documentation can be searched, and is fairly easy to understand, especially if you have a basic knowledge of WordPress, so if you need help you should easily find what you are looking for.

If you are using a particular plugin or theme, and require help for it, check the documentation and website for the plugin/theme developer, which may include additional help.

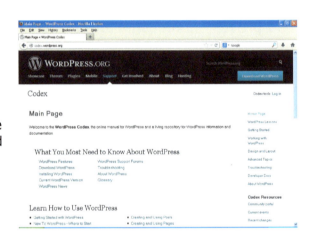

Forums

There are also support forums for WordPress where you can ask questions:

www.wordpress.org/support

Before posting a new question, you may wish to search the forum to see if your question has already been asked and answered. Before posting on any forum check any guidelines for posting, ensure you post in the correct section and provide as much information as possible.

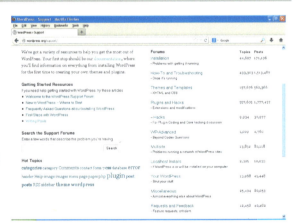

Learning about advanced topics

This book has focused mainly on the management aspect of a WordPress website, and less on advanced topics (e.g. creating and modifying themes, etc.)

If you would like to learn more about the technical details of WordPress, or any of the software it uses, for example MySQL or PHP, then there are a range of books from various publishers covering these advanced topics. You will also find a lot of documentation and information on the Internet, including the WordPress website.

Other sources of help

Check with your web designer/developer whether they can offer any support and assistance.

There are also third party websites, forums, etc. that offer support on using WordPress.

If you are stuck on a particular area of WordPress, search the Internet (e.g. using Google) for WordPress and the subject which you wish to find more information about.

You could also look for YouTube videos and podcasts.

Looking for help with your WordPress website? Author Simon Pittman is happy to consider opportunities for freelance web work – either on a one-off or ongoing basis – to discuss further, e-mail: **simon@libraryplayer.co.uk**

Also by the Author

Editing Audio Using Audacity
2018 (Second Edition)
Whether you are new to editing audio or have used similar software packages, this book will get you started in using Audacity to edit your audio, and point you in the right direction to finding further information and help.

How to Develop Software
2015
Whether you are interested in learning about how software is developed or interested in a career, this book will help you get started. Illustrated with examples, and using a language with English-style statements, this book will help you start to understand the concepts and ideas involved with developing software. *Now available on Kindle!*

Looking for help with your membership? Struggling with your todo lists? Looking for an easier way to launch applications on your computer?

Simon Pittman develops a range of software products – find out more (and download free trials) at:
www.libraryplayer.co.uk
www.pittlaunch.co.uk

Involved with a club, charity or voluntary group?

Receive help and support running your organisation – join the **Member Manager Plus** group for free at:
facebook.com/groups/MemberManager